1066 &
The Battle of Hastings
in a Nutshell

1066 &
The Battle of Hastings in a Nutshell

Copyright © 2017
MadeGlobal Publishing

ISBN-13: 978-84-946498-5-1

M
MadeGlobal Publishing

For more information on
MadeGlobal Publishing, visit our website:
www.madeglobal.com

Cover Illustration: The Battle of Hastings *by* Anthony Hillman © 2017 Anthony Hillmand and MadeGlobal

For my parents, who have nurtured and
encouraged my interest in history from an
early age and have put up with my obsession
and non-stop talking about it since.

xx

Contents

Durham ●

● Stamford Bridge
York ●
● Riccall

$\left[\right.$ 25miles / 40km

● Lincoln

Derby ● ● Nottingham

● Northampton

England

Tower of London ●

Senlac Hill/Battle Abbey
Pevensey, Castle ● ● Hastings
Eastbourne

Isle of Wight

Timeline

1042 – Edward the Confessor becomes King of England

1051 – Edward possibly promises the throne to William of Normandy

1053 – Godwin dies and his son Harold becomes Earl of Wessex

1057 – Edgar Ætheling arrives back in England

1064 – Harold visits Normandy and possibly swears an oath to William

1065 – Northumbrians revolt against Earl Tostig

January 1066 – King Edward dies and Harold becomes King of England

25 September 1066 – The Battle of Stamford Bridge

28 September 1066 – William lands at Pevensey

14 October 1066 – Duke William of Normandy defeats King Harold at Hastings

25 December 1066 – William I crowned at Westminster Abbey

1071 – Harrying of the North

1086 – The Domesday Survey records England's land holdings and economic assets

9 September 1087 – Death of William I. William II (Rufus) becomes King of England

Introduction

The Battle of Hastings in 1066 has been named as one of the most important events in English history. In fact, for some people, it may be the only date in history they know. Many recall the story of William sailing over from Normandy, going to battle with the newly proclaimed King Harold and the latter supposedly dying of an arrow to the eye. Few know the details of why the battle happened and even fewer know what happened afterwards, during the reign of William the Conqueror.

The year 1066 brought about the arrival of the Normans and the demise of the Anglo-Saxon way of life in England. Some of the physical manifestations – the motte-and-bailey (wooden castles on great mounds) followed by castles made in stone – still survive. But this is just the tip of the iceberg of many changes the new king brought to England.

This book aims to explain how the Battle of Hastings came about, to dispel some of the popular myths and to examine the aftermath of the battle.

Re-enactors at Battle Abbey, near the site of the engagement, celebrate this event every year, but should we really glorify 1066? A year in which the English were conquered – a year when many of the old governing class were supplanted by the Conqueror's men. Some argue that pre-conquest England had been a much nicer place – freer and more liberal.

In this book, I aim to provide a balanced account on whether, in the broad sense, the Norman Conquest was a good thing for England, to fill in some of the blanks and to dispel some of the common myths.

Edward, Harold and William
The Succession Crisis

The story begins in 1042 with Edward, known as the Confessor, peacefully taking the English throne after years of turmoil. Edward was a direct descendant of Alfred the Great and thus had always been destined for the throne, yet this, for a time, was not certain. Edward's father, Athelred II, had been overthrown by King Sweyn of Denmark and his son Canute. Edward fled into exile and his mother remarried King Canute, giving him two sons. It must have seemed like a miracle when, in 1035, Canute died and his two sons, Harold and Harthacanute, followed him to death in quick succession. This left Edward to peacefully take the throne, yet he could not have imagined that England would again be in turmoil after his death.

Edward the Confessor married the daughter of a prominent nobleman, Earl Godwin, who had risen to power during Canute's reign. His new queen, Edith, also had two brothers, the most important ones in this story being Harold (later King Harold II)

and Tostig. The family were seen as upstarts, having no royal blood. They were simply the in-laws of the new king. The Earl was also implicated in the murder of Edward's brother and controlled the king, who was still finding his feet in a country largely unknown to him.

Earl Godwin died in 1053 and Harold and Tostig inherited the bulk of his estates. The Godwins had, by then, gained control of most of England, with only Mercia having escaped their grasp. The Domesday Book shows that the family estates amounted to around £7,000 in 1066, with Harold's share at £5,000. No other family came close to this amount, including the king, whose estates stood at £5,000.

However, despite the relative peace during his reign, King Edward would remain childless, leading to the events of 1066. Six years into their marriage, he and Edith still had no children, leading Edward to take actions to secure the succession. Why they were childless has been debated by historians, with some saying the marriage was unconsummated due to Edward's piety and others proposing that they had slept together but there were fertility problems. Whatever the case, in a council of March 1051, Edward announced that he wanted his heir to be William of Normandy (later, the Conqueror).

William of Normandy, or, as he was known at the time, William the Bastard, was the illegitimate son of Robert I, Duke of Normandy. William was related to King Edward through Edward's mother, Emma of Normandy, and William's great-aunt. William had met Edward during the prince's exile on the Continent and so may have given him some support when he returned to England. Therefore, to William, it may not have been a surprise when Edward made him his heir, despite his claim not being the strongest.

However, the suggestion that Edward promised William the throne occurs only in Norman sources written, or at least revised, after the Norman Conquest itself. This has led some historians to doubt that the promise was ever made at all, and to argue that it was simply a story dreamt up after the event to justify William's accession. It is still not unlikely that Edward promised him the throne at this time – especially when we take into account the next events.

Sometime in the spring of 1064, Harold made a trip to France – an event which is shown in the opening section of the Bayeux Tapestry. It is one of the most debated events of the time, for in spite of it being included in the Tapestry and also in chronicles written in Normandy, the contemporary English sources are silent on the matter. There is, however, little doubt that the visit is a true story. All versions – both contemporary Norman and later English – agree in broad outline about what happened.

William of Poitiers, Duke William's chaplain, provides a detailed Norman view of the visit:

> *'About the same time (1064), Edward King of the English, who had already established William as his heir and whom he loved as a brother or a son, gave a guarantee more important than anything hitherto. He resolved to forestall the inevitability of death, for whose approaching hour this holy man, seeking heaven, made ready. To confirm his promise by a further oath he sent to him Harold, of all his subjects the greatest in riches, honour and power...'*[1]

This account suggests that Harold agreed to go to William on Edward's behalf to confirm his status as the king's heir. In reality, we cannot be sure whether or not Harold really did set on Edward's behalf, there are conflicting accounts that suggest he instead wanted to free his brothers, who had been taken as hostages.

---

1. *Gesta Guillelmi ducis Normannorum et regis Anglorum (The Deeds of William Duke of Normandy and King of England)*, ed. R. H. C. Davis and M. Chibnall (1998), Oxford, p70-71

'At a council convened at Bonneville Harold publicly swore fealty to him by the sacred rite of Christians. And according to the entirely truthful relation of certain most notable men of utter integrity who were present at the time, at the end of the oath he freely added the following clauses; that he would be the agent of Duke William at the court of his lord King Edward as long as the latter lived; that he would strive with all his influence and power to bring about the succession of the English kingdom to William after Edward's death [2]

This account does have to be viewed cautiously as William of Poitiers was close to the duke and needed to justify the later actions of his master. According to this version, Harold was travelling on Edward's behalf to confirm the offer of the English throne to Duke William. En route he was shipwrecked and held captive by the Count of Ponthieu for ransom, before being rescued by William and taken to his court. While there, Harold took an oath of loyalty to William. Of his own free will, William of Poitiers asserts, he also promised to help the duke secure the English throne on Edward's death. The Bayeux Tapestry provides a visual account of this story including the crucial oath-taking scene.

It is hard to fully accept this version of events because it seems highly unlikely that Harold would have been prepared to make such a trip and offer. As the most powerful man in a country, a man that lacked a direct heir and as a king in all but name, Harold may well have been casting his own eyes on the throne by this stage. There is also no corroboration of William of Poitiers' version of the story in the two main English sources, the *Anglo-Saxon Chronicle* and *Vita Ædwardi Regis*.

One later source argues that, rather than going to confirm Edward's promise to William, Harold went to secure the release of two of his nephews and his brother from William. While in

---

2. Ibid.

William's court, the oath was then extorted from Harold. This can be supported by a later account by Eadmer, who states that he did indeed take the oath under duress: *'He could not see any way of escape without agreeing to all that William wished'*[3]. He had been freed from imprisonment by William who also held members of his family captive and so he might only have been able to escape from Normandy by agreeing to William's demands. If this were the case, according to the standards of the day, the oath would not have been binding.

Whatever the truth, this oath would later come back to haunt Harold. By 28 December 1065, the date in which Edward was to attend the dedication ceremony at his Westminster Abbey, the king was dying. The *Vita Ædwardi Regis,* an account dedicated to Edward's queen, describes his last moments in great detail, evoking the images of the king as a saint:

> *'Let us describe how this gem of God stripped off the corruption of his earthly body and obtained a place of eternal splendour in the diadem of the heavenly king. When he was sick unto death and his men stood and wept bitterly, he said 'Do not weep, but intercede with God for my soul, and give me leave to go to Him'… Then he addressed his last words to the queen who was sitting at his feet, in this wise, 'May God be gracious to this my wife for the zealous solicitude of her service. For she has served me devotedly, and had always stood close by my side like a beloved daughter. And so from the forgiving God may she obtain the reward of eternal happiness.*[4]

What makes this account vital to the story of the Battle of Hastings is what it implies when Edward speaks to Harold. It is a little vague in what Edward actually asks of Harold, but it could be interpreted in a few different ways:

---

3. *Eadmer's History of Recent Events in England,* ed. G. Bosanquet (1964), p.7-8
4. *Vita Ædwardi Regis*

'And stretching forth his hand to his governor, her brother, Harold, he said, 'I commend this woman and all the kingdom to your protection. Serve and honour her with faithful obedience as your lady and sister, which she is, and do not despoil her, as long as she lives, of any due honour got for me. Likewise I also commend those men who have left their native land for love of me, and have up till now served me faithfully.' [5]

According to this account, Edward commended *'all the kingdom'* [6] to Harold's protection, which could easily be interpreted as Edward appointing him as his successor. This mattered as, according to the standards of the time, a dying man's last words were the most solemn that could be spoken. This meant that Harold's claim took precedence over any other.

On 5 January 1066, Edward died and was buried in Westminster the next day. The leading magnates and clergy (known as the Witan) met on the same day as the funeral to discuss and confirm Harold as King of England. They would have discussed the strengths of Harold, other claimants, and the dangers posed by outsiders. It is probable that Edward's dying words would have been given prominence at the meeting. The outcome is, of course, known - Harold was crowned later the same day.

The Norman sources viewed Harold's actions as a betrayal and that his coronation had no legitimacy. Once again, William of Poitiers documents the duke's reaction to the news:

'And now unexpectedly there came a true report, the land of England was bereft of her king Edward, and his crown was worn by Harold. Not for this insane Englishmen the decision of a public choice, but, on that sorrowful day when the best of kings was buried and the whole nation mourned his passing, he seized

---

5. Ibid.
6. Ibid.

the royal throne with the plaudits of certain iniquitous supporters and thereby perjured himself. He was made king by the unholy consecration of Stigand, who had been deprived of his ministry by the justified fervour of papal anathema. Duke William took counsel with his vassals and determined to avenge the wrong by arms and in arms to claim his inheritance, although many magnates argued persuasively against the enterprise as too hazardous and far beyond the resources of Normandy.[7]

Some historians view Harold's actions as one of undue haste, especially with his coronation being on the same day as the previous king's funeral, yet this is not so. The Witan had chosen him as king and he knew that he needed to act as soon as possible. This was due to threats not just from Duke William, but also from the Scandinavian kings and his own brother, Tostig.

Tostig had been exiled by his brother several years previously. After being appointed Earl of Northumbria in 1055, Tostig attempted to bring the region under control, but in doing so he acquired a reputation as a tyrant. He employed brutal tactics and funded his efforts by raising taxes. The fact that he was a Southerner ruling over the fiercely independent North only added to his unpopularity. It proved too much when Tostig arranged the murder of three local magnates and, in 1065, the Northumbrians rose up against him. Tostig's household was slaughtered, his treasure plundered and Morcar, son of Earl Aelfgar of Mercia, was installed as the new earl. The rebels then began to march south, sacking Lincoln, Nottingham, Derby and Northampton and threatening the stability of England. The king then placed Harold in charge of finding a solution, resulting in Morcar being formally elected as earl and Tostig being sent into exile. Tostig fled to Flanders, vowing revenge on his brother.

---

7. *Gesta Guillelmi ducis Normannorum et regis Anglorum (The Deeds of William Duke of Normandy and King of England)*, ed. R. H. C. Davis and M. Chibnall (1998), Oxford, p100-1

Tostig's opportunity of revenge on Harold came in 1066 when, after making a joint invasion pact with Harald Hardrada (a Viking), who had a slim claim himself to the throne, he arrived on the Isle of Wight. With a fleet of 60 vessels, he pillaged the south and east coasts, before sailing into the protection of Scottish waters. It had not been successful, as losses and desertions left Tostig with only 12 ships.

Calculating that Normandy, instead of Norway, was the real danger and believing the defence of the North could be left to the earls, Edwin and Morcar, Harold chose to base his forces on the south coast. Throughout the summer, his navy made regular patrols, hoping to intercept and potentially destroy the Norman fleet. It did not appear. Unfavourable winds kept William at bay and on 8 September, with supplies running low and having kept his forces in the field for an unprecedented four months, Harold was forced to demobilise. This is recorded in the *Anglo-Saxon Chronicle*:

> *'Earl Tostig came from overseas into the Isle of Wight was as large a fleet as he could muster and both money and provisions were given him. And then he went away from there and did damage everywhere along to sea-coast wherever he could reach until he came to Sandwich. When King Harold, who was in London, was informed that his brother Tostig had come to Sandwich, he assembled a naval force and a land force larger than any king had assembled before in this country, because he had been told as a fact that Count William from Normandy, King Edward's kinsman, meant to come here and subdue this country.'*

Harold had already been preparing an army for when William arrived – so the arrival of Tostig was well prepared for – yet there was one drawback to the king's new army. Most of the men who made up the force were only obliged to give a few months labour to the king and, with Harold keeping them on watch for an invasion from Normandy, they soon had to leave for the year:

> '*Then King Harold came to Sandwich and waited for his fleet there, because it was long before it could be assembled; and when his fleet was assembled, he went to the Isle of Wight, and lay there all that summer and autumn; and a land force was kept everywhere along by the sea, though, in the end, it was no use. When it was the Feast of the Nativity of St Mary [8 September], the provisions of the people were gone and nobody could keep them there any longer. Then the men were allowed to go home, and the king rode inland, and the ships were brought up to London.*[8]

A week later and powered by the same wind that had curtailed William, Harald Hardrada arrived off the coast of north-west *east* England. His 300 longships joined Tostig's much smaller fleet in rowing up the River Ouse before disembarking at Riccall. Their destination was the old Viking stronghold of York, about sixteen kilometres away. Tostig had promised that the North would rally to their banner, but at Gate Fulford, about 3 kilometres short of their target, Edwin and Morcar's men formed up and blocked the road. It was 20 September and the first of the year's three great battles was about to begin.

To the right flank of the English army lay the river, with marsh to the left. Numbers stood at around 6,000 men apiece, all on foot. The battle commenced with a Saxon charge into the Viking right under the command of Tostig, successfully pressing it back. Experience now told and Hardrada sensed an opportunity. He wheeled his left forces around and smashed into the side of the advancing English. After a short but intense fight, the Saxons broke and in trying to escape the pincer movement many lost their lives in the marsh. In truth, the outcome was not surprising. Edwin, the eldest at around 18, and Morcar were both

---

8. *Anglo-Saxon Chronicle, A.D. 1066, Abingdon Manuscript C.*

inexperienced. They faced hardened warriors well used to fighting together and a leader of exceptional quality. The battle cost the English around 1,000 lives. Although both northern earls lived to fight another day, they now had no immediate capacity to supply Harold with fresh troops.

An Icelandic historian, poet and politician, writing in the 13th century, offers an account of these events:

> 'King Harald lay in the Ouse when the army of the earls (Edwin and Morcar) came down from the land to oppose him. Then the king went on land and began to array his army for battle. One wing stood on the bank of the river, the other was arrayed further up on land, and extended to a ditch. There was a swamp, deep and broad and full of water. The earls deployed their army down along the river with the whole body of their men. The royal banner was close by the river. There the king's men stood thickest, and the lines were thinnest by the ditch, with the troops he could least rely on. Then the earls proceeded down along the ditch. There the wing of the Norwegian army extending to the ditch gave way, and the English followed them up, thinking that the Norwegians were about to flee. That part of the English army was led by Morcar.'[9]

This detailed account is one of the few we have of the first of the three battles in the year 1066, sounding credible despite it being written over a hundred years after the event. The author of the account placed much value on gathering sources of his own and viewing his work critically, yet the account is often forgotten. He goes on to explain how Harald Hardrada faced the English Earls:

---

9. *The Saga of Harald Sigurtharson,* Snorri Sturluson

> 'But when King Harald saw that the battle array
> of the English had come down along the ditch right
> opposite them, he had the trumpets blown and sharply
> urged on his men to the attack, raising his banner
> called Landwaster. And there so strong an attack was
> made by him that nothing held against it. Then there
> was a great slaughter among the earl's men. Soon their
> army took to flight. Some fled up or down along the
> river, but most leapt into the ditch. There the bodies of
> the fallen lay so thick that the Norwegians could walk
> dry-shod over the swamp.'[10]

With a credible Norman threat, Harold also knew the Vikings had to be stopped and he quickly began raising a replacement army. Collecting his men in London, he commenced a forced march on the old Roman road of Ermine Street and covered a spectacular three hundred kilometres in five days. On the way, his numbers were swelled by native recruits. It had been a daring strategy because it risked wearying his men, however, Harold needed to stop Hardrada from having the chance to consolidate his hold. He was also planning on taking the Vikings by surprise. Reaching Tadcaster, about twenty-four kilometres from York, late on 24 September, Harold heard the enemy was camped at Stamford Bridge and decided to attack following day.

The first the Vikings knew of the Anglo-Saxon's presence was an approaching cloud of dust. By then, the Anglo-Saxons were around one and a half kilometres away. The element of surprise worked – several Vikings didn't even have their protective mail coats on. The fighting that followed was ferocious; with an initial delaying action by a small cluster of Vikings on the west bank of the river Derwent, the task eventually falling to a lone Viking on the bridge himself – where he cut down around forty Anglo-Saxons single-handed. Once the Anglo-Saxons were through onto the east bank, the main phase occurred on the ground currently

10. *Ibid.*

referred to as Battle Flats. The Norsemen formed a traditional shield wall and a battle of attrition ensued as the Anglo-Saxons launched sustained attacks. It was during this stage that Hardrada was taken down by an arrow to the throat. The ultimate phase was entered once Viking reinforcements arrived from Riccall where they had been protecting the fleet. This brought an initial boost – however, by nightfall the Viking shield wall had disintegrated and they were being ruthlessly hunted down.

Although precise numbers are not known, Harold definitely had the advantage. This was probably in the order of two to one as Hardrada made the fatal mistake of dividing his forces by leaving a significant part to guard his fleet. Once these reinforcements did arrive, they were exhausted after a march in full kit. In terms of equipment and tactics, though, each side was very similar, fighting on foot in a shield wall with the battle-axe as the weapon of choice. The loss of Hardrada so early on in the battle was a severe blow. Tostig was killed soon after.

The Battle of Stamford Bridge deserves to be better known. The forced march and surprise attack portrayed outstanding military ability. It was one of the heaviest defeats suffered by the Vikings at the hands of the English and it put an end to any further Norse invasions. It is said that a whole century after the battle, unburied Viking bones still littered the site.

Significantly, one day after the battle, the wind shifted and therefore the Norman fleet could depart. Landing four hundred kilometres to the south at Pevensey, Harold now had to face his most dangerous opponent with an exhausted and depleted army.

The Battle of Hastings

Duke William is not given much credit for the immense logistical task of mustering his invasion force. His first task was to secure the backing of the nobility. Many needed persuading, believing that it was too dangerous and far beyond the resources of Normandy. Through force of personality and promise of great rewards, he won them over in a series of assemblies. Meanwhile, as part of a diplomatic assault, a formal protest was sent to Harold, while the Norman case was set out before Pope Alexander by Lanfranc, abbot of St Stephen in Caen. Although the exact details are not known – probably a case of perjury on Harold's part – we do know that the Pope was convinced and sent William his papal banner as his blessing. This mattered because the venture now had the support of the head of the Church. Soldiers from outside Normandy – especially from Brittany, Ponthieu and Flanders – flocked to join his banner, also lured by the promise of riches and William's outstanding military reputation.

An account – probably drawn up in the abbey of Fecamp – details the contributions of ships and soldiers made by William's magnates in 1066:

> 'When William, duke of the Normans, came to England to acquire the throne, which by right was owed to him, he received from William FitzOsbern the steward sixty ships; from Hugh, who later became earl of Chester, the same; from Hugh of Montfort fifty ships and sixty soldiers; from Remigius, almoner of Fecamp who later became bishop of Lincoln, one ship and twenty soldiers; from Nicholas, abbot of Saint-Ouen fifteen ships and one hundred soldiers; from Robert, count of Eu, sixty ships; from Fulk of Anjou forty ships; from Gerald the steward the same number; from William, count of Evreux eighty ships; from Roger of Montgomery sixty ships; from Roger of Beaumont sixty ships; from Odo, bishop of Bayeux, one hundred ships; from Robert of Mortain one hundred and twenty ships; from Walter Giffard thirty ships and one hundred soldiers. Apart from these ships, which all together totalled one thousand, the duke had many other ships from his other men according to their means. The duke's wife Matilda, who late became queen, in honour of her husband had a ship prepared called 'Mora' in which the duke went across. On its prow Matilda had fitted a statue of a child who with his right hand pointed to England and with his left hand held an ivory horn against his mouth.'[11]

By August, William's fleet was ready, lying off Dives-sur-Mer, while an army of perhaps 10,000 men lay in camp. It has been calculated that to maintain this force for one month would have required 9,000 cartloads of food and fuel. The 2,000 warhorses alone would have needed 13 tonnes of both grain and hay a

---

11. *The Ship Lists of William the Conqueror*

day. It is, therefore, a significant achievement that William kept his army provisioned from around August to October without the need to pillage the surrounding countryside. William also seems to have avoided the other curses of large military encampments: ill discipline and disease. In September, he moved his fleet to the mouth of the River Somme, to exploit the shorter crossing, and then waited for a favourable wind.

The fleet of ships arrived off the shingle beach at Pevensey on the morning of 28 September. Landing on hostile terrain, the success of the whole enterprise now depended on William's military leadership and judgement. His first steps onto English soil could not have been more inauspicious. Stumbling, William loudly proclaimed to his aghast soldiers that he was seizing England with both hands, as related by William of Poitiers. In truth, William could not have been luckier. Had he landed earlier in the summer, he would have been met with immediate resistance. From Pevensey, William quickly moved to Hastings, which had the benefit of a large harbour as well as a defensible location in the event of a retreat. Strategically astute, William knew that it was in his interest to fight a tired Harold quickly, and in a place of his choosing. A long delay would open up problems of provisioning and maintaining morale. At its worst, William could find himself facing winter blockaded in the Hastings peninsula by the Saxon fleet on one side and a reformed Saxon army on the other. William's plan was simple, to tempt Harold into early battle. William, therefore, sent his armies to ravage the surrounding lands, which formed part of Harold's Wessex earldom. The Bayeux Tapestry shows houses and huts being burnt to the ground while terrified occupants cower outside.

The *Anglo-Saxon England* volume of the *Oxford History of England* series details the logistics of Harold's travel south and how long the news would have taken to reach him:

'The distance from Pevensey to York is 250 miles in round numbers. Without the aid of beacons, of which there is no tradition, the news of William's landing on the morning of 28 September can hardly have reached York before the evening of 1 October. The march from London into Sussex must have begun on 11 October. Even if the preparation of the summonses was taken in hand at York on 2 October, at least a day must have been required for their completion and dispatch. Within the eight days between 3 and 11 October it was impossible for the ordinary thegns of remote counties to receive their summonses from the sheriff, prepared themselves for war, and ride to London. The difficulty is no less if it is assumed that the writs were dispatched from London, for Harold can scarcely have reached the city before 6 October.'[12]

The choices Harold now made in response to William's provocation would provide the context in which the Battle of Hastings was fought. The new king did not hesitate. From York, he raced his army down the old Roman road of Ermine Street again, stopping on the way at his foundation of Waltham Abbey to pray for victory. He covered the 305 kilometres in eight days. Five days were spent in London gathering what forces he could before a further 110 kilometres forced march south took him to the enemy. Harold's decision to force an early confrontation can be seen as reckless in the extreme and the result of his personal desire to avenge the damage done to his Wessex lands. While Harold can be seen as falling into William's trap, there is some rationale to his decision. He did not know whether William was receiving reinforcements from the continent and so growing stronger by the day. As lord and king, he felt morally bound to help his subjects. It also presented Harold with attractive military options. He may have been thinking of launching a Stamford Bridge style surprise

---

12. Stenton, Frank. *Anglo-Saxon England (Oxford History of England)*, p592

attack or else bottling William up in the Hastings peninsula, where he would soon run out of supplies. Both scenarios required him to move fast. Ultimately, though, it was a poor choice. It meant that Harold arrived for battle with exhausted troops and, crucially, his reinforcements were still on their way. A few more days would have resulted in a much more formidable army, including the archers he was forced to leave behind at Stamford Bridge, as well as Edwin and Morcar's men. In addition, he could have brought his fleet to bear by cutting off William's supply lines. William's plan had, however, worked and these options were closed down.

Late on Friday, 13 October, the Saxon arrival in the Hastings peninsula was spotted by Norman scouts, removing Harold's option of a surprise attack. Both sides knew the morning would bring battle. Norman sources claim the Saxons spent that night drinking and feasting and the Normans in silent prayer. There is little truth in this. Instead, like all soldiers preparing for battle, it would have been a tense and nervous time. At first light, initial manoeuvring saw Harold occupy the high ground on Senlac Hill. For William, the challenge was clear. For him to march on London and secure the crown, Harold had to be removed from the hill and defeated that day. For Harold, a simple draw would suffice.

Harold formed his army up along the crest of the ridge occupying a front just under one kilometre in length. At the crown lay his own position and the two standards – the Dragon of Wessex and the Fighting Man. Although estimates vary, his army probably stood at between 7,000 and 8,000 men. His infantry was organised in ten ranks, all on foot, with the well-armed and equipped men at the front, forming a protective shield wall and assuming the place of greatest danger. Behind them were men lightly armed with a spear or battle-axe and shield.

Harold's plan seems to have been to hold this strong position where the Norman cavalry would be least effective and take any opportunities they were offered. He spoke to his men, stressing their invincibility if they stood firm.

Shouting the English war cry of 'Ut, ut' ('Out, out') and beating their shields, these troops – now fired for battle – were able to look down the slope towards the assembling Normans. The Norman army was similar in size but contained a higher proportion of professional fighting men. It also had a very different composition. William placed his archers and crossbowmen in the front line, then the heavy infantry in chain mail tunics carrying spears and at the rear the elite knights on warhorses. This reflected the sequence of planned attack. William also divided the army into three divisions. On the left were the Bretons, in the centre the Normans and on the right the French. Finally, William placed himself at the centre, armed with a mace and riding his Spanish warhorse *'so that he could direct operations on all sides with hand and voice'*[13], as William of Poitiers writes. William warned his men that retreat was impossible and defeat meant death. He spoke of Harold's broken oath and reminded them that God was on their side and the pope had blessed their crusade. Alongside him flew the papal banner.

Senlac Hill would, therefore, see a clash between two very different armies. The Anglo-Saxons represented the old guard, fighting on foot in the style of the Vikings. This had disadvantages. In particular, it was hard for a leader on foot truly to command his army once battle had commenced, although his presence in the battle line must have boosted the morale and fighting spirit of his men. The Norman use of mounted knights and archers represented the future of medieval warfare and these assets would prove crucial in William's ultimate victory. However, it is wrong to assume that the outcome was inevitable. Both armies were capable of carrying the day. Although Harold was weakened by the loss of so many trained fighters at Stamford Bridge and limited in his ability to command, he had the advantage of holding the high ground – the shield wall was extremely powerful

---

13. *Gesta Guillelmi ducis Normannorum et regis Anglorum (The Deeds of William Duke of Normandy and King of England)*, ed. R. H. C. Davis and M. Chibnall (1998), p126-7

in defence and he did not need to deliver a knockout blow. In order to determine the outcome at Hastings, it is necessary to look at the course of the battle and in particular the decisions made by the two commanders.

The battle began at nine in the morning, with an aggressive plan of attack from William. While his strategy of ceaselessly taking the fight to Harold would ultimately lead to victory, it took time to bring results. Archers fired into the shield wall but the line held firm. William then sent his infantry up the slope. Brutal hand-to-hand fighting ensued but still the English line refused to break. It also held out against the first assault by cavalry. William of Poitiers stated that the English *were so tightly packed together that there was hardly any room for the slain to fall*[14]. This pattern of attack continued for several hours before reaching a crisis point at around noon. The Bretons broke, fleeing back down the slope in the face of mounting losses. Sensing victory, some of the English poured down after them. To avoid becoming isolated and also in response to the spreading panic, the centre and right of William's line also began to pull back. Rumour then spread that William himself had been killed. The Norman army was on the cusp of collapse. It was at this point that leadership on both sides played a critical role. Harold failed to capitalise on the ensuing Norman chaos by ordering a general charge. The potential to sweep the Normans from the hill was lost. On the other side, William, pushing back his helmet, rode across his troops showing them that he was alive. The Norman line began to solidify and then turned on the now isolated Englishmen. Here the difference in the troops in the two armies became evident, as outside the protection of the shield wall the more poorly armed and armoured men were no match for the Norman knights, who cut them down with relative ease.

By now it was around 2pm. Both sides paused to reform and then William once more sent his infantry and cavalry up the slope

---

14. Ibid.

and fighting resumed. Due to the steep sides, flanking or going around the enemy was not an option and direct assaults on the shield wall continued. The Normans began using the tactic of feigned retreats to weaken the shield wall. This claim has generated intense controversy among historians, with some debating whether they were actually deliberate. It is likely that after the almost retreat – when the rumour spread that William was dead – they used this to their advantage. As a result, the actions of William's cavalry were responsible for significantly degrading Harold's forces. They would also help deliver the final blow. William of Poitiers describes these retreats in his account:

> 'The Normans and their allied forces, realising that they could not overcome an enemy so numerous and standing so firm without great loss to themselves, retreated, deliberately feigning flight. They remember how, a little while before, flight had been the occasion of success. The barbarians exulted with the hope of victory. Exhorting each other with triumphant shouts, they poured scorn upon our men and boasted that they would all be destroyed then and there. As before, some thousands of them were bold enough to launch themselves as if on wings after those they thought to be fleeing. The Normans, suddenly wheeling their horses about, cut them off, surrounded them, and slew them on all sides, leaving not one alive.'[15]

Barbarians at the time meant foreigners, but still Poitiers' account is very judgemental in what he sees as the subjects of William fighting against their lawful king. As well as this, they were fighting against a cause supported by the Pope, putting their souls in jeopardy by supporting a usurper.

---

15. Ibid.

> 'Twice they used the same stratagem to the same
> effect, and then attacked more furiously than ever
> the remaining enemy, still a formidable force and
> extremely difficult to surround. It was now a strange
> kind of battle, one side attacking with all mobility,
> the other enduring, as though rooted to the soil. The
> English began to weaken, and as if confessing their
> guilt by their submission, suffered the punishment.
> The Normans shot, smote and pierced: it seemed as if
> more movement was caused by the falling dead than
> by the living. Those who were only wounded could not
> withdraw, but died in the press of their companions.
> Thus fortune sped to accomplish William's triumph.'[16]

At about 4pm with light fading and the shield wall severally weakened, William's leadership skills again came to the fore. He had the determination to rally his troops and order one last assault to break the enemy line. He coordinated this last attack so that his archers fired high in order to ensure the arrows would land on top of the Anglo-Saxons. His cavalry, followed by infantry, then smashed through the shield wall. William was in the thick of the fighting and narrowly escaped death, losing his third horse that day. King Harold was not so lucky and his death saw English resistance crumble. Loyalty meant some of the men gathered around their dead king and went down fighting. Elite losses that day included Harold's two brothers, Gyrth and Leofwine. The once-mighty Godwin family had collapsed completely.

William's victory at Hastings is due to a combination of factors. The challenge is to decide where the balance lies. Was the battle won by the Normans or lost by the Saxons?

William's victory stemmed from his careful preparation. While in Normandy he built up a broad coalition of support, ranging from Norman magnates to the pope. His logistical organisation was meticulous, allowing an army to be maintained in the field

16. Ibid.

throughout the summer and then successfully transported across the Channel. Once in England, William chose to stay in a defensive pocket and ravaged land to provoke Harold into battle. The strategy paid off. It was William – rather than Harold – who picked the time and place of battle, helping neutralise Harold's natural advantage of fighting on home soil. This superior generalship, honed by a youth campaigning in France, came to the fore during the battle. William took the fight to Harold and throughout the day relentlessly attacked. He saw the potential for victory in the chaos of the Breton retreat and proved his skill in rallying wavering troops. William of Poitiers once again gives an overview of the battle:

> 'In 1066, a huge army from all provinces in England gathered together at Hastings in order to unjustly defend their land. For a long time the battle raged furiously. The English profited by remaining in their shield wall, the superiority of their numbers and the effectiveness of their weapons. Thus they bravely withstood the Normans. Realising they could not overcome an army in such close formation, the Normans faked a retreat and the English barbarians, thinking victory within their grasp, gave rapid pursuit. But the Normans suddenly wheeled their horses, surrounded them and cut them down. They repeated this twice. At last the English began to weary and, as if confessing their crime in their defeat, submitted to their punishment.'[17]

Harold's rush to engage William also meant that he threw away all the advantages that stemmed from his position as the sitting king and leader of the Godwin family. Waiting would have allowed Harold to assemble an overwhelming army but by not taking the long view, Harold faced William with an under-strength force, lacking experienced men. The folly of this became apparent when

---

17. Ibid.

the untrained peasants repeatedly broke the shield wall during the feigned retreats. During the battle, Harold lacked inspiration. He did not order a general charge but nor was he able to keep his army on the hill in their defensive position, which would have allowed him to see the day out. *The Chronicle of Florence of Worcester* gives a brief account of Harold's actions:

> *'Although King Harold knew that some of his best troops had fallen in the two previous battles and that half his army had not yet arrived, he advanced and met his enemies nine miles from Hastings. But many of the English left the ranks and very few remained true to him. Nevertheless, from the third hour of the day until dusk, they bravely withstood the enemy and fought so well and so stubbornly that the Normans could make little impression. At last, about twilight, after great slaughter on both sides, the king fell.'*[18]

As well as these factors, William gained a decisive edge in the battle from his heavy cavalry and archers. Furthermore, Harold was severely limited in his ability to command his troops by fighting on foot in the Viking style. Compare this with William's horse-borne prominence, which allowed him to rally his troops following the Breton collapse. However, the outcome of the battle should not be viewed as inevitable. Despite the undoubted advantage that William's highly trained and mobile force gave him, the battle was a close-run thing until the key moment of Harold's death.

Many died and the scale of this is demonstrated by a passage in *The Battle Abbey Chronicle*:

---

18. *The Chronicle of Florence of Worcester*

'there was exhibited a fearful spectacle: the fields were covered with dead bodies, and on every hand nothing was to be seen but the red hue of blood. The dales all around sent forth a gory stream which increased at a distance to the size of a river'[19]

The death and violence of the Battle of Hastings have left no visible trace nor have relics of the battle ever been found on what is thought to be the battlefield. This has led to some dispute over whether it was actually fought there at all, with some citing what is now a roundabout, around 600ft from the Abbey instead. Either way, Battle Abbey is where Harold died, with modern researchers confirming this – although 20ft to the east of the original memorial stone.

Early tradition recorded that, just before the Battle of Hastings, Duke William made a vow to establish a monastery on the site of the battle if God granted him victory. This story however only appears for the first time in a forged charter of 1154. It is more probable that William's vow was the result of penances imposed by the papal legates in 1070. Like a great war memorial, the foundation of Battle Abbey could be seen to honour the dead as well as to be a public act of atonement by the King for the bloodshed of the Conquest. In addition, such a grandiose project fitted the Normans' intention of constructing highly visible buildings that represented their power and authority and emphasised the permanency of the Conquest. Situating an abbey on the battlefield would also attract settlers to a comparatively empty stretch of country that had only recently proved to be a good invasion route. In naming it Battle Abbey, the Normans demonstrated their self-confidence and a degree of arrogance.

---

19. *The Battle Abbey Chronicle*, ed. E. Searle (1980)

An Arrow to the Eye?

What ultimately decided the Battle of Hastings was the death of King Harold, but how did Harold die? The established story, as most know it, is that the king was felled by an arrow that hit him in the eye. The Bayeux Tapestry famously shows Harold gripping the arrow that had lodged in his face, and this is seemingly backed up by several chroniclers, however this version has recently been debated.

The Bayeux Tapestry was probably commissioned in the 1070s by Bishop Odo of Bayeux, half-brother of William the Conqueror. It was probably made in England, not Bayeux, and by the English, which may mean there was a conflict of interest over the depiction of events.

There is debate over which figure is actually Harold in this scene of the Tapestry. Is he the upright figure grasping the arrow – whose head, after all, interrupts the word 'Harold' in the caption – or is he the falling figure immediately to the right, being hacked down by a horseman, under the words '*interfectus est*' ('was killed')? Also, even if we accept that the first figure represents

Harold, there is controversy over the arrow itself. The Tapestry was heavily restored in the mid-nineteenth century, and the death of Harold is one of the areas where the restorers may have taken considerable liberties. Some experts contend – from an analysis of the embroidery and an examination of the earliest drawings of the Tapestry in its apparently unrestored state – that the first figure is actually holding not an arrow but a spear, ready to hurl at his attackers.

We also have to consider the fact that the Tapestry is our only contemporary source to suggest that Harold was hit in the face by an arrow. The *Carmen*, William of Poitiers, William of Jumieges and the various versions of the *Anglo-Saxon Chronicle* make no mention of it. In the case of the last two, this omission is not very remarkable, given the brevity of their accounts; in the case of William of Poitiers and the *Carmen* it is altogether more striking. Poitiers offers us the longest and most detailed account of the battle, yet makes no mention of the manner in which Harold died. Possibly this was because he did not know. Alternatively, it may have been because he knew full well, having read the *Carmen*'s version, and did not care to endorse it.

For the *Carmen* – our earliest source for the battle – offers an entirely different account of how Harold met his end. According to the account, the battle was almost won – the French were already seeking spoils of war – when William caught sight of Harold on top of the hill, hacking down his foes. The duke called together a cohort of men and set out to kill the king. In this they were successful, and the *Carmen* gives us a graphic description of the injuries each inflicted on Harold, who was pierced with a lance, beheaded with a sword and disembowelled with a spear. His thigh, we are told – possibly a euphemism for his genitalia – was hacked off and carried away some distance.

William of Poitiers silence on the subject is telling. In general, he is not afraid to contest points of detail with the *Carmen* and offer his own version of what happened. When it comes to Harold's gory end, however, he offers no denial and no alternative scenario.

Poitiers wanted to present the duke as measured, merciful and just in all his dealings, and in particular in his pursuit of England's throne. He did not want to show his hero, whose mission had been sanctioned by the pope, hacking his opponent into pieces. The credibility of the *Carmen* is enhanced by the fact that the poem's author, Guy of Amiens, had close connections with the men he tells us were William's accomplices.

We know that at various points in the battle, the Normans showered the English with arrows and crossbow bolts – so it is not unlikely that Harold was hit, perhaps fatally, perhaps in the eye. At the same time, we cannot lightly disregard the *Carmen* when it tells us that Harold died in a very different way, deliberately cut down by his enemies. Apart from anything else, a deliberate killing accords well with William's assumed war-aim. He had risked everything to get an army to England and to bring Harold to battle. After a long day's fighting, with the autumn light starting to fade, it would have been quite possible for the English king to withdraw, enabling him to fight another day. William would not quit. An anonymous arrow in the eye accorded better with the idea that, in the final analysis, Harold's death had been down to the judgement of God.

As William of Poitiers and several other sources make clear, Harold's corpse was in a very bad state, stripped of all its valuables, and so hacked about the face that it could only be recognised by 'certain marks'. According to the twelfth-century tradition at Waltham Abbey, the task of confirming his identity required the presence of Harold's partner, Edith Swan-Neck:

*'She had at one time been the king's concubine and
knew the secret marks on his body better than others
did, for she had been admitted to a greater intimacy
of his person. Thus they would be assured by her
knowledge of his secret marks when they could not be
sure from his external appearance.'* [20]

In contemporary accounts, by contrast, it is the king's mother,
Gytha, who appears to plead for the return of her son's body.
Despite allegedly offering its weight in gold, her request was
refused. William angrily replied that it would be inappropriate
for Harold to be interred while countless others lay buried on
his account.

---

20. *The Waltham Chronicle: An Account of the Discovery of Our Holy Cross and Its
    Conveyance to Waltham*

Aftermath of the Battle

Unlike modern assumptions, the English people were initially very resistant to the change in kingship. *The Anglo-Saxon Chronicle* describes how William the Conqueror expected England to submit to him fairly easily; however he was to be disappointed:

> 'William the earl went afterwards again to Hastings, and there awaited to see whether the people would submit to him. But when he understood that they would not come to him, he went upwards with all his army which was left to him, and that which afterwards had come from over sea to him; and he plundered all that part which he over-ran until he came to Berkhampsted. And there came to meet archbishop Aldred [of York]... and Edwin the earl, and Morcar the earl, and all the chief men of London; and then submitted, for need, when the most harm had been done: and it was very unwise that they had not done so before; since God would not better it, for

our sins: and they delivered hostages, and swore oaths
to him; and he vowed to them that he would be a
loving lord to them: and nevertheless, during this, they
plundered all that they over-ran. [21]

As described, William destroyed land in the South as
he headed towards London before confronting the leading
Englishmen to force them to submit. Some, such as William of
Poitiers, argue that the destruction was accidental since William's
men had to forage for food and supplies as they went. However,
others argue that it was to destroy Harold's old lands and any hope
of possible resistance from the Southerners. John of Worcester
even explicitly writes that the Norman *'laid waste Sussex, Kent,*
Hampshire, Middlesex, and Hertfordshire, and did no cease from
burning townships and slaying men [22].

Hearing of this, the Englishmen resigned themselves to the
fact that they had a new Norman king. He was quickly crowned:

'Then, on midwinter's day, archbishop Aldred
consecrated him king at Westminster; and he gave
him a pledge upon Christ's book, and also swore,
before he would set the crown upon his head, that he
would govern this nation as well as any king before
him had at the best done, if they would be faithful
to him. Nevertheless, he laid a tribute on the people,
very heavy; and then went, during Lent, over sea to
Normandy, and took with him archbishop Stigand,
and Alynoth, abbat of Glastonbury… and Edwin the
earl, and Morkar the earl, and Waltheof the earl, and
many other good men of England. And bishop Odo

21. *The Anglo-Saxon Chronicle,* ed J.A. Giles (1914), p139
22. *The Chronicle of John of Worcester,* ed. RR. Darlington and P. McGurk,
    vol II, p606-7

and William the earl remained here behind, and they built castles wide throughout the nation, and poor people distressed; and ever after it greatly grew in evil. May the end be good when God will![23]

On Christmas Day 1066, William was crowned King of England in a ceremony deep in symbolism. Taking place at Westminster Abbey and following an order of service that dated back to the coronation of King Edgar in 973, William needed to reinforce the point that he was the true heir and successor of King Edward. Once he was anointed by archbishop Ealdred of York, he also gained the aura of being blessed by God, so he could now tap into the Anglo-Saxon's inherent loyalty to the Crown, regardless of its wearer. The coronation, however, showed just how insecure the Normans felt. Mistaking English shouts of approval for William as signs of revolt, the guards panicked and set fire to nearby houses and fighting broke out outside the Abbey itself.

Despite some small rebellions scattered around the country, the greatest threat to William's rule came from the North and he would be forced to take to the field three times in extended campaigns between 1068 and 1070. Having been restored to a number of their lands in 1067, Edwin and Morcar soon realised that, despite William's initial promises to rule in conjunction with the Anglo-Saxon elite, in reality, they wielded little power and influence. Edwin felt personally embittered that William had broken a promise to marry one of his daughters to him. William, aware that resistance was starting to build in the North – centred on York – acted to head off trouble. He staged a series of raids into Warwickshire, Nottinghamshire and Yorkshire, blazing a trail of destruction. As the Anglo-Saxon Chronicle says, *'he allowed his men to harry [attack/destroy] wherever they came'* and *'slew many hundred persons'*. The policy worked. He received the surrender of Edwin and Morcar and established a castle in York before returning southwards.

---

23. *The Anglo-Saxon Chronicle*, ed J.A. Giles (1914), p139-40

If 1068 had been difficult for William, 1069 was crucial. In January, rebels attacked Durham, killing the Norman Earl Robert of Commines and his knights. The news quickly spread to York, where local insurgents lay siege to the castle. In a lightning march reminiscent of Harold's advance on Stamford Bridge, William was able to relieve the garrison at York. After establishing a second castle in a clearly troublesome town, William returned south to celebrate Easter at Winchester.

Events once again spiralled out of control in the summer, when a Danish fleet of 240 ships containing an army of trained warriors appeared off Kent. It was led by King Sweyn's sons, Harold and Canute. The appeals of the grieved English people had finally borne fruit. The fleet raided its way up the east coast of England before anchoring off the River Humber. Yorkshire now descended into rebellion and the Danes seized York in September. This was the most dangerous point for William. He was not facing a rebellion in a fiercely independent region which resented rule from the South, as the rebellion against Tostig in 1065 demonstrated. William reacted with speed and brutality and headed north. He staged a march from Nottingham to York, devastating the land as he went before reoccupying the city for a third time. He also went in search of the Danish army but they refused to give battle. William celebrated Christmas amid the empty, burnt-out ruins of York. To show his authority, he wore the crow, which had been specially brought up from Winchester. William then undertook one of the most brutal acts of his reign and arguably the one that had the most devastating effect on the English people, the Harrying of the North.

William split his troops up into smaller warbands and they set about the systematic destruction – or harrying – of Yorkshire and the surrounding areas.

According to the usually restrained *Anglo-Saxon Chronicle* the king went '*with all his army that he could collect, and utterly ravaged and laid waste to that shire*[24]. Orderic Vitalis' account, written around 1114, when it was safer to voice criticism, gives a more vivid insight into the scale of violence:

> *'He [King William] himself continued to comb forests and remote mountain places, stopping at nothing to hunt out the enemy hidden there. His camps were spread over an area of 100 miles. He cut down many in his vengeance; destroyed the lairs of others; harried the land and burned homes to ashes. Nowhere else had William shown such cruelty. Shamefully he succumbed to this vice, for he made no effort to restrain his fury and punished the innocent with the guilty. In his anger he commanded that all crops and herds, chattels and food of every kind should be brought together and burned to ashes with consuming fire so that the whole region north of Humber might be stripped of all means of sustenance. In consequence, so serious a scarcity was felt in England, and so terrible a famine fell upon the humble and defenceless populace, that more than 100,000 Christian folk of both sexes, young and old alike, perished of hunger.'*[25]

This was a bleak time for the English and even the chroniclers, who normally supported William, found that they could not support this. Orderic Vitalis finds that he has to explain this in his account:

> *'My narrative has frequently had occasion to praise William, but for this act which condemned the innocent and guilty alike to die by slow starvation I cannot commend him. For when I think of helpless children, young men in the prime of life, and hoary*

24. *The Anglo-Saxon Chronicle*, ed J.A. Giles (1914), p146
25. *Historia Ecclesiastica*, Orderic Vitalis

greybeards perishing alike of hunger, I am so moved to
pity that I would rather lament the grief and sufferings
of the wretched people than make a vain attempt to
flatter the perpetrator of such infamy.[26]

The region did not recover for generations. In 1086, the Domesday Book designated one-third of Yorkshire as 'waste' – meaning uninhabitable. The Battle of Hastings may not have had a direct effect on the people of the North like the Battle of Stamford Bridge did, however the change in kingship did. The English had grievances with the fact that William was replacing the majority of the English elite with Normans, many close companions or family of the new king.

William the Conqueror was also meticulous in how he governed his land. Due to the chaos of the change in kingship, there were many land disputes, mainly due to William promising two different people the same land. Wanting to know everything about his new kingdom and to settle these land disputes, he commissioned the Domesday survey. The Domesday survey attempted to address this problem by acting as a judicial inquiry. *The Anglo-Saxon Chronicle* once again documents William's actions and how Domesday was commissioned:

> 'The king had great thought and very deep conversation
> with his council about this land, how it was occupied,
> or with which men. Then he sent his men all over
> England into every shire and had them ascertain how
> many hundreds of hides there were in the shire, or
> what land and livestock the king himself had in the
> land, or what dues he ought to have in 12 months
> from the shire. Also he had it recorded how much
> land his archbishops had, and his diocesan bishops,
> and his abbots and earls, and – though I tell it at
> too great length – what or how much each man had
> who was occupying land here in England, in land or

---

26. *Ibid.*

in livestock, and how much money it was worth. He had it investigated so very narrowly that there was not one single hide, not one yard of land, not even (it is shameful to tell – but it seemed no shame to him to do it) one ox, not one cow, not one pig was left out, that was not set down in his record. And all the records were brought to him afterwards.[27]

During its process of investigation, special courts were held in each county and the people were asked to verify the various details collected by the commissioners. As well as this, they were also asked to state who owned the land. Disputes were common at this stage but the verdicts recorded by Domesday became definitive. As such this document acted as a charter of confirmation, giving the great landowners legal security over their estates. William symbolically marked its completion at an extraordinary ceremony within the confines of an old Iron Age fort at Salisbury. The great landholders paid homage to him and swore oaths of loyalty. In so doing, they confirmed the principle that William was the ultimate source of all tenure in England.

The survey/book is an invaluable primary source for modern historians. No survey approaching the scope and extent of the Domesday Book was attempted again in Britain until the 1873 Return of Owners of Land – sometimes called the Modern Domesday – which presented the first complete, post-Domesday picture of the distribution of property in the British Isles. This was a huge feat for the time and did result in a period of calm due to fewer land disputes.

An example from the Domesday Book, about a town (the author's hometown) that was near the battle site:

'In Bexhill Hundred
Osbern holds Bexhill from the Count [of Eu]. Before
1066 Bishop Alric held it because it is the bishoprics;
he held it later until King William gave the castelry

---

27. *The Anglo-Saxon Chronicle,* ed J.A. Giles (1914), p156-7

HISTORY "In a Nutshell" SERIES

of Hastings to the Count. Before 1066 and now it answered for 20 hides. Land for 26 ploughs. The Count [of Eu] holds 3 hides of the lands of the manor himself in lordship. He has 1 plough; 7 villagers with 4 ploughs. Osbern has 10 hides of this land; Venning 1 hide; William of Sept-Meules less ½ virgate; Robert St. Leger 1 hide and ½ virgate; Reinbert ½ hide; Ansketed ½ hide; Robert of Criel ½ hide; the clerics Geoffrey and Roger 1 hide in prebend; 2 churches. In lordship 4 ploughs; 46 villagers and 27 cottagers with 29 ploughs. In the whole manor, meadow, 6 acres. Value of the whole manor before 1066 £20; later it was waste; now £18 10s; the Count's part 40s thereof. Osbern holds 2 virgates of land from the Count [of Eu] in this Hundred. It always answered for 2 virgates. He has 5 oxen in a plough. The value was 8s; now 16s.[28]

The knights in William's army were rewarded with land in England after the Conquest – often after taking it away from their previous landowners. For example, the Bexhill manor was owned by the bishops of Chichester but William took it away and gave it to Robert Count of Eu. The phrase 'later it was waste' may suggest that Bexhill was destroyed during the Norman Conquest. It may have been destroyed while William was moving his army between Pevensey and Hastings, going through Bexhill and destroying it in the process. However, it is more likely that the Norman army raided the surrounding countryside after taking over Hastings – as they did with other parts of the South. This was to prevent local uprisings and, if done before the battle, would have influenced Harold's decision to move his army South.

The Anglo-Saxon Chronicle describes the Norman king's reign, briefly detailing the various laws in which he imposed and how the English people felt:

---

28. *Domesday Book Vol 2: Sussex*, ed by John Morris, p9-11

'He had castles built and wretched men oppressed. The King was so very stark and seized from his subject men many a mark of gold, and more hundreds of pounds of silver that he took by weight, and with great injustice from his land's nation with little need. He was fallen into avarice, and he loved greediness above all. He set up great game-preserves, and he laid down laws from them, that whosoever killed hart or hind he was to be blinded. He forbade hunting the harts, so also the boards; he loved the stags so very much, as if he were their father; also he decreed for the hares that they might go free. His powerful men lamented it, and the wretched men complained of it but he was so severe that he did not care about the enmity of all of them; but they must wholly follow the king's will if they wanted to live or have land – land or property or his good favour.'

Of course *The Anglo-Saxon Chronicle* was not going to support a Norman taking the English throne, even lamenting about how he has sinned for taking the throne and how he treated the English people:

'Alas, woe, that any man should be so proud, raise up and reckon himself over all men. May the Almighty God show mercy to his soul and grant forgiveness of his sins.'[29]

William the Conqueror built many castles in England, which were mainly to help subdue and intimidate the English – who vastly outnumbered the Norman people. Many of these still survive today, the most notable of which being the Tower of London. Before he reached London, after the Battle of Hastings, William of Poitiers records the new king ordering the advance guard to build a fortress in the city, *'as a defence against the*

---

29. *The Anglo-Saxon Chronicle*, ed J.A. Giles (1914), p161

inconstancy of the numerous and hostile inhabitants[30]. The Tower was not actually begun until the 1070s, on the site William originally selected in 1066, and remained unfinished at the time of his death. It was only eventually completed during the reign of his son. As this implies, the result was a truly monumental building, three storeys high, a royal palace that would overawe the populace of the kingdom's principal city. Construction on this scale had not been seen in Britain since the days of the Roman emperors whom William was so eager to emulate.

Other than the Tower of London, William built castles in places where he thought there would be the most resistance to his rule (as seen in the North). Castles were essentially introduced to England by the Normans and defined the Conquest:

> '*The King rode into all the remote parts of his kingdom and fortified strategic sites against enemy attack. For the fortifications called castles by the Normans were scarcely known in the English provinces so the English in spite of their courage and love of fighting could put up only a weak resistance to their enemies.*'[31]

The English people were not experienced in castle warfare and so were unable to tackle the Normans and their castles. Despite occasional stirrings of rebellion, they were unable to overthrow the new Norman dynasty.

William I died on 9 September 1087, having atoned extensively the weeks previously for his sins and what he inflicted on the English people. He had commanded that his treasure be distributed among the poor and divided up among the various churches. He also attempted to please God by ordering the release of all the prisoners in his custody.

Upon hearing of the king's death and fearing his successor, the wealthier men rode off as quickly as they could to protect their

---

30. *Gesta Guillelmi ducis Normannorum et regis Anglorum (The Deeds of William Duke of Normandy and King of England)*, William of Poitiers
31. *Historia Ecclesiastica*, Orderic Vitalis

properties, leaving the lesser attendants to loot the royal lodgings. Weapons, vessels, clothing and furnishings – all were carried off, says Orderic Vitalis in his chronicle. By the time the frenzy was over, all that remained was the king's body lying almost naked on the floor.

Since all the royal attendants had fled, there was nobody left to make the required arrangements for the late king's funeral; in the end a humble knight named Herluin paid out of his own pocket to have the body prepared and transported by boat. A distinguished crowd of bishops and abbots had assembled outside St Stephen's Abbey to lay the king to rest, and the bishop of Evreux preached a long and eloquent sermon, extolling William's many virtues. He concluded by asking the assembled crowd to forgive their former lord if he had ever done them any harm and an aggrieved local man stepped forward to complain in a very loud voice that the land they were standing on had once belonged to his father, and had been violently taken by the conqueror in order to provide for the abbey's foundation. Claiming the land for his own, he forbade the ceremony to go any further. After a headlong enquiry established that he was telling the truth, the man was appeased by an immediate cash payment and the service continued. However, the greatest insult was reserved until last. Once William was finally lowered into the ground, it became clear that his bloated body was too big for the stone coffin, and efforts to press on regardless caused his swollen bowels to burst. No amount of perfumes or spices could hide the stench, and the clergy, therefore, raced through the remainder of the ceremony before rushing back to their homes.

Orderic reminds us that William had been a powerful and warlike king, feared by many people in various lands, yet in the end, he was left naked and needing the charity of strangers. Perhaps this was his true retribution for the violence and bloodshed he brought to England.

The Bayeux Tapestry

The Bayeux Tapestry contains some of the most memorable images documenting the Battle of Hastings. However, it is not really a tapestry, it is an embroidery. One reason that has been suggested for this now incorrect name is that the original meaning of the word 'tapestry' only meant a 'hanging'. The designs on the Bayeux Tapestry are embroidered, yet nonetheless, it will forever referred to as a tapestry.

It is a piece of embroidered cloth of nearly seventy metres (230 feet) long and fifty centimetres (20 inches) tall, and depicts the events leading up to the Norman Conquest of England, focusing specifically on William, Duke of Normandy, and Harold, Earl of Wessex, culminating in the Battle of Hastings.

The tapestry consists of around fifty scenes with Latin *tituli* (inscription), adorned on linen with coloured woollen yarns. It is likely that it was commissioned by Bishop Odo, William's half-brother, and was made in England in the 1070s. It was rediscovered in Bayeux and appeared to have been there for several years, hence the name.

The tapestry can be seen as the final and best-known work of Anglo-Saxon art, and though it was made after the Conquest, it was made in England, firmly following Anglo-Saxon tradition.

The long strip of linen is formed of nine bands sewn together. It is difficult to find any trace of the initial drawings in the places where the thread has now disappeared; the Tapestry must originally have been outlined, maybe on a separate pattern, with nothing left to improvisation.

The embroidery is sewn with two-ply wool yarn; the main stitches used are stem stitch and laid-and-couched work. All the outlines and the stunning inch-high letters of the inscriptions are sewn with stem stitch. Where there is the colour of skin, the linen is left bare.

The earliest known written reference to the tapestry is in a 1476 inventory of Bayeux Cathedral, however its origins are the topic of much speculation and controversy. French legend maintained the tapestry was commissioned and created by Queen Matilda, William the Conqueror's wife, and her ladies-in-waiting. Indeed, in France it is often referred to as *La Tapisserie de la Reine Mathilde* (Tapestry of Queen Matilda). However, a scholarly analysis in the twentieth century concluded it was probably commissioned by William's half-brother, Bishop Odo, who, after the Conquest, became Earl of Kent and, when William was absent in Normandy, Regent of England.

There are many reasons as to why scholars think Odo commissioned the Tapestry. One is that three of the bishop's followers mentioned in the Domesday Book appear on the tapestry. Another is that it was found in Bayeux Cathedral which was built by Odo and another is that it may have been commissioned at the same time as the cathedral's construction in the 1070s – probably completed by 1077 in time for display on the cathedral's dedication.

Assuming Odo commissioned the tapestry, it was probably designed and constructed in England by Anglo-Saxon artists – Odo's main power base being in Kent – and the Latin text contains hints of Anglo-Saxon. Other embroideries of this era also tend to originate from England and therefore the dyes used can be found in cloth traditionally woven there.

The Tapestry ends with Harold being slain; however, this was not initially the end of their story. The last part of the tapestry is missing but it is thought that the story contained only one extra scene.

In its approximately fifty scenes, a scholar has counted that the Tapestry depicts 623 human figures, 202 horses, 55 dogs, 505 other creatures (such as birds and beasts), 37 buildings, 41 ships and boats, 49 trees and nearly 2,000 letters beside these.

The reason the Bayeux Tapestry occupies a quite unique position among pictorial hangings of the period is partly that it is so large and so incredibly well-preserved, and partly that it depicts a series of historical events well-known from literature, which it is able to confirm, and indeed in some cases to supplement. The invaluable significance of the Bayeux Tapestry lies, among other things, in its vivid and elaborate representation – thought often stylised and at times almost naïve – of a number of the features of both daily life and warfare which gave shape to human existence at a point in time which can be precisely dated. For Scandinavians these pictures possess a special interest in that they show conditions and objects which in several cases correspond closely to those of their own culture during the late Viking age.

Selected scenes from the Bayeux Tapestry[32]

Figure 5 - UBI HAROLD SACRAMENTUM FECIT
WILLELMO DUCI
(Where Harold made an oath to Duke William)

In this scene we see Harold swearing on holy relics to uphold a promise to William. The problem is that we do not know what Harold is swearing to exactly, and under what conditions. The Normans would have us believe Harold is swearing to uphold William's claim to England although we do not know the terms he swore to. Harold could also be swearing under duress, thus meaning he had no obligation to uphold it once he arrived back in England.

---

32. Translation compiled from several works: Mogens Rud's *The Bayeux Tapestry* (2004) and Frank Stenton's *The Bayeux Tapestry* (1965). Verified with the SPQR application. Images from http://www.hs-augsburg.de/~harsch/Chronologia/ Lspost11/Bayeux/bay_tama.html

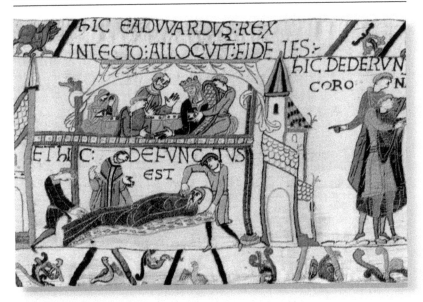

Figure 6 - HIC EADWARDUS REX IN LECTO
ALLOQUIT[UR] FIDELES
ET HIC DEFUNCTUS EST
(Here King Edward in bed speaks to his
faithful followers and here he died)

Here we see Edward the Confessor on his deathbed, a moment important for both the Normans and the English. It can be interpreted several ways, the most common one being that Edward is nominating Harold, one of the men surrounding him, as his successor.

Figure 7 - HIC RESIDET HAROLD REX ANGLORUM
STIGANT ARCHIEP[ISCOPU]S
(Here sits Harold King of the
English Archbishop Stigand)

Here we see Harold as King of England, along with Archbishop Stigand. The Normans would later argue that Stigand had no authority to crown him, seeing as he was guilty of simony, the buying or selling of the church lands. While it is true that Stigand was guilty of this, in reality, he actually only performed the funeral services for Edward and did not crown Harold – this right went to Ealdred, the Archbishop of York. Therefore this scene is a form of propaganda made to reinforce William's claim to the throne and undermine Harold's kingship.

Figure 8 - HIC WILLELM[US] DUX IN MAGNO NAVIGIO
(Here Duke William in a great ship sailed)

Figure 9 - MARE TRANSIVIT
(across the sea)

Figure 10 - ET VENIT AD PEVENESAE
(and came to Pevensey)

These scenes above show William crossing the sea to England and landing at Pevensey, in Sussex.

Figure 11 - HIC HAROLD REX INTERFECTUS EST
(Here King Harold is slain)

This is one of the most well known sections of the Tapestry, showing a scene depicting Harold's death. For many years it was said that Harold was slain by an arrow in the eye (second man on the left). However, most historians now agree that this is a later addition and instead suggest that Harold is the man being trampled by a Norman on horseback (furthest right).

Other Claimants

It is not well known that in 1066 there were alternative claimants to the throne after King Edward had died, not just Harold and William. However, due to reasons which will now be explored, they are hardly mentioned by historians and ultimately these other claimants were discarded for the likes of Harold.

Arguably, the person with the strongest claim to the throne was Edgar Ætheling, grandson of Edmund II, who was the only candidate for the throne who could trace his descent directly from an English king – both Harold and William were only related to Edward the Confessor through marriage. Edgar was born before 1057, maybe in 1052, and almost certainly in Hungary, where his father, Edward Ætheling, finally found refuge from Canute's attempts to eliminate him. King Canute needed to eliminate any potential rivals to the throne, but he did not achieve this as both father and son survived. They were brought back to England in 1057, once Edward the Confessor had become king. Edward Ætheling was Edward the Confessor's nephew and, when he died, there were even some rumours that he was poisoned by

Harold's family, the Godwinsons. It hints that the family wished to take the throne, however there is no evidence to support these rumours. If they did wish to take the throne, then why was the young Edgar not removed also? There are too many questions to take this claim seriously.

According to the *Leges Edwardi Confessoris* (*Laws of Edward the Confessor*), the young Edgar was given the name 'Ætheling', which means 'throneworthy'[33], by the king, his great-uncle, Edward the Confessor. Since Edgar was not the son of a king, this was apparently a political statement by the childless King Edward regarding the succession. However, other sources suggest that Edward was not considering Edgar, presumably because he was too young – being in his early teens in 1066 – and because he had been brought up in a foreign country. Edgar also had no powerful kin to promote him and to resist Harold, who was the dominant figure in English politics and also the most powerful man in the kingdom.

Interestingly, after Harold's demise at the Battle of Hastings, rather than submitting to William, the English people turned to Edgar. In London, Archbishop Ealdred of York and the citizens wanted to have Edgar as their king, according to a version of the *Anglo-Saxon Chronicle* which displays a particular interest in Edgar and his family:

> 'Archbishop Aldred and the townsmen of London would then have child Edgar for king, all as was his true natural right: and Edwin and Morcar vowed to him that they would fight together with him.'[34]

There is some evidence that Edgar's claim was taken seriously outside London. The Abbot of Peterborough died shortly after Hastings and the monks chose as his successor, Brand, sending him to Edgar for confirmation:

---

33. *Leges Edwardi Confessoris (Laws of Edward the Confessor)*, ed F. Liebermann (1903), p665
34. *The Anglo-Saxon Chronicle*, ed J.A. Giles (1914), p139

> '*Then chose the monks for abbat Brand the provost, by reason that he was a very good man, and very wise, and sent him then to Edgar the etheling, by reason that the people of the land supposed that he should become king: and the etheling granted it him then gladly. When king William heard say that, then was he very wroth, and said that the abbat had despised him.*'[35]

At first, the earls Edwin and Morcar promised Edgar their support, but soon submitted to William instead. Edgar was never crowned, and, without the backing of the two most significant surviving earls, his cause was hopeless. In early December, he himself submitted to William I at Berkhamsted, along with several bishops and earls. He was awarded land and honours and was treated as one of William's dearest companions, at least according to William of Poitiers, whose intention was always to flatter his master. Whether or not this is true, what is most striking about William's treatment of Edgar is that he allowed him both life and freedom, in stark contrast to Canute's behaviour towards the English royal family after his conquest of England in 1016.

For reasons that are unclear – although it may have been due to the promise of power but having none, similar to Edwin and Morcar – Edgar and his family left England for the court of King Malcolm III of Scotland in 1068. Then, early in 1069, he was at the head of the Northumbrian rebels who entered York and, following their defeat by William, he fled back to Scotland. In the late summer, a large Danish fleet arrived in the Humber Estuary, and Edgar and other northern nobles joined them in rebellion. Despite seeming like they would win for a time, there was still no indication that the Danish would make Edgar their king. The Danish king, Sweyn, soon concluded an agreement with William, leaving the English rebels in the lurch, and yet again Edgar withdrew to Scotland. After a brief expulsion from Scotland – because of William's invasion there – Edgar

---

35. *The Anglo-Saxon Chronicle*, ed J.A. Giles (1914), p142

HISTORY "In a Nutshell" SERIES

eventually submitted to William I and was established at his court. William of Malmesbury, writing in 1125, bitterly criticised Edgar's behaviour, *'remaining at court for many years, silently sunk into contempt through his indolence, or more mildly speaking, his simplicity*[36]. He alleges that Edgar gave up his daily stipend of a pound of silver in return for a single horse. The Domesday Book reveals that Edgar held two estates in Hertfordshire in 1806 – at Barkway and Hormead. Having settled down to an easy life in the end, nobody would have guessed he had once been the strongest claimant to the English throne.

The other claimant to the English throne has already been explored a little already – Harald Hadrada. The King of Norway, born in 1015, had pursued many claims to different kingdoms but, after peace negotiations with Denmark in 1064, he turned to England. Harald claimed that, as the successor to the Danish kings (including Canute), he had a legitimate claim to the English throne. This was a weak claim at best and, unlike the other claimants, Edward the Confessor had never acknowledged this. Harald saw an opportunity to pursue this claim when the disgruntled Tostig arrived in Norway to support him, yet still found himself defeated by King Harold at the Battle of Stamford Bridge in 1066.

---

36. *De Gestis Regum Anglorum*, ed. John Sharpe (1815), p325

Should we celebrate the Battle of Hastings?

Over recent years, there has been much criticism of people celebrating the Battle of Hastings with re-enactments, family events and even special commemorative coins being released for the 950th anniversary. But should we really be celebrating the date on which we were conquered by the Normans?

The Battle led to massive defeat on the English side, with many dead, and with the land in the South being devastated by William's army before and immediately after Harold met William at Hastings. William then later essentially destroyed the North, which took years to recover, with the Harrying of the North.

The Norman Conquest changed the English language forever and, for a time, the dominant language in England was actually French. English itself only came back into literature in 1215, with the signing of Magna Carta, and even then it was not the same English that had been spoken before. It was not the same England.

Words had been changed, many of which we still use now, such as calling an animal a pig but the meat pork. Here are some examples:

Anglo-Saxon	Norman
Cow	Beef
Sheep	Mutton
Kingly	Royal
Brotherly	Fraternal
Ask, Beseech	Enquire
Inn	Tavern

As well as the words, England's aristocracy, its attitudes and its architecture had all been transformed by the coming of the Normans. Many of the buildings and architectural styles still survive, such as the stone towers of Dover, Rochester and The Tower of London.

Despite the rebellions – and some of William's intimidating tactics towards the English – both the English and Normans did eventually learn to tolerate each other and soon we hear stories of intermarrying between the two very different people:

> 'English and Normans were living peacefully together in boroughs, towns and cities and were intermarrying with each other. You could see many villages or town markets filled with displays of French wares and merchandise and observe the English, who had previously seemed contemptible to the French in their native dress, completely transformed by foreign fashions.'[37]

So should we celebrate the Battle of Hastings? No, we should not celebrate the event itself, with the many dead and some of the subsequent actions by the new king. However, it did lead to a new way of life for the English, a new culture and, having made castle

---

37. *Historia Ecclesiastica*, Orderic Vitalis

building popular in England, architecture that would help the people withstand later invasions.

Myths and Facts about the Norman Conquest

Myth 1: Edward the Confessor was very religious

Edward the Confessor was no more religious than the average person in Medieval England. The confusion stems from two facts; the fact that Edward didn't have children and that he was later canonised. Edward was married to Queen Edith for several years, yet they produced no children, leading later ecclesiastical writers to claim that this was because Edward took a vow of celibacy. However, this is dismissed by modern historians. In the view of Edward's biographer, Frank Barlow, *'the theory that Edward's childlessness was due to deliberate abstention from sexual relations lacks authority, plausibility and diagnostic value*[38]. Despite whatever religious views he may have had, he would have known that his duty as king was to provide an heir.

---

38. *Edward the Confessor.* Frank Barlow (1997), p82

In 1051, Godwin and his sons fell out with Edward and fled the country. Edith was sent to a nunnery, possibly because she was childless, and Edward hoped to divorce her. This could also support the fact that he was not celibate and possibly even aimed to remarry. However, this was not to be. When the Godwins came back to power, Edith was reinstated as queen.

Edward the Confessor was the first Anglo-Saxon and the only King of England to be canonised. With his proneness to fits of rage and his love of hunting, Edward is regarded by most historians as an unlikely saint, and he was canonised for political reasons, although some argue that his cult started so early that it must have had something credible to build on.

After 1066, there was a subdued cult of Edward as a saint, which gradually increased in the early 12th century. Osbert of Clare, the Prior of Westminster Abbey, then started to campaign for Edward's canonisation, aiming to increase the wealth and power of the Abbey. By 1138, he had converted the *Vita Ædwardi Regis*, the life of Edward commissioned by Edith, into a conventional saint's life. He seized on an ambiguous passage which might have meant that their marriage was chaste, perhaps to give the idea that Edith's childlessness was not her fault, to claim that Edward had been celibate. In 1139, Osbert went to Rome to petition for Edward's canonisation with the support of King Stephen, but he lacked the support of the English hierarchy and Stephen had also quarreled with the church, so Pope Innocent II postponed the decision, declaring that Osbert lacked sufficient testimonials of Edward's holiness.

In 1159, there was a dispute election to the papacy, and Henry II's support helped to secure recognition of Pope Alexander III. In 1160, a new Abbot of Westminster, Laurence, seized the opportunity to renew Edward's claim. This time, it had the full support of the king and the English hierarchy, and a grateful pope issued the bull of canonisation on 7 February 1161. This was more to do with the combined interests of Westminster Abbey, King Henry II and Pope Alexander, than to do with Edward's piety. He was called 'Confessor' as the name for someone who was believed to have lived a saintly life but was not a martyr.

Myth 2: Very little happened after the Norman Conquest, the new king was quickly accepted

As shown in this book, the English did not easily accept William. This is a common misconception and may be due to the fact that many know about the Battle of Hastings but not what came after it, such as the Harrying of the North.

In reality, England becoming peaceful, quickly, after the event of 1066, is far from true. A large period of adjustment was in order, not helped by William's initial destruction of the South and the replacement of a large proportion of the English nobility. England arguably did not have a prolonged period of peace until the reign of Henry I, which was, even then, still followed by the Anarchy.

Places of Interest

Battle Abbey and Battlefield

The battlefield in which Harold and William's armies fought in 1066, with Harold dying where the high altar of the abbey once stood is well worth a visit. The Abbey itself was founded by King William in 1071, and was established as a memorial to the dead of the battle and as atonement for the bloodshed of the Conquest. It was also a highly visible symbol of the piety, power and authority of the Norman rulers.

Opening Times: 10:00 – 18:00 daily
http://www.english-heritage.org.uk/visit/places/1066-battle-of-hastings-abbey-and-battlefield/

Figure 1 - Battle Abbey © Philip Halling

Figure 2 - Site of the battle © Malc McDonald

Pevensey Castle

Pevensey Castle is the landing place of William the Conqueror's army in 1066. It was originally a Roman fort in the 4th century AD. After the Conquest, a full-scale Norman castle, with a great square keep and a gatehouse, was built within one corner of the fort.

Opening Times: 10:00 – 18:00 daily
http://www.english-heritage.org.uk/visit/places/pevensey-castle/

Figure 3 - Pevensey Castle © Paul Farmer

Tower of London

The impressive fortress which William the Conqueror commissioned to dominate the landscape and intimidate the English people has become known as the Tower of London. Though many later kings and queens stayed at the Tower, it was never intended as the main royal residence. Its primary function was as a fortress and stronghold, a role that remained unchanged right up until the late 19th century. It was extended by later rulers, adding outside walls and more defences, but the main Norman structure in the centre (the White Tower) still survives to this day.

01 November – 28 February (Winter)
Tuesday – Saturday: 09:00 – 16:30
Sunday – Monday: 10:00 – 16:30
Last Admission: 16:00
01 March – 31 October (Summer)
Tuesday – Saturday: 09:00-17:30
Sunday – Monday: 10:00-17:30
Last Admission: 17:00
http://www.hrp.org.uk/tower-of-london/

Figure 4 - The White Tower © Tim Ridgway

Bibliography

Primary Sources:

The Anglo-Saxon Chronicle, ed J.A. Giles (1914)

Leges Edwardi Confessoris (Laws of Edward the Confessor), ed F. Liebermann (1903)

Vita Ædwardi Regis

The Waltham Chronicle: An Account of the Discovery of Our Holy Cross and its Conveyance to Waltham

Historia Ecclesiastica

Gesta Guillelmi ducis Normannorum et regis Anglorum (The Deeds of William Duke of Normandy and King of England), ed. R. H. C. Davis and M. Chibnall (1998), Oxford

The Chronicle of Florence of Worcester

The Battle Abbey Chronicle, ed. E. Searle (1980), Oxford

The Ship Lists of William the Conqueror

Sturluson, Snorri. *The Saga of Harald Sigurtharson*

The Chronicle of John of Worcester, ed. RR. Darlington and P. McGurk

Domesday Book Vol 2: Sussex, edited by John Morris

De Gestis Regum Anglorum (On the Deeds of the Kings of the English), ed. John Sharpe (1815)

Secondary Sources:

Wise, Terence (1979). *1066 Year of Destiny,* Osprey Publishing
Who's Who in the Middle Ages Volumes 1-2 (2006), Routledge
Morris, Marc (2013). *The Norman Conquest,* Windmill Books
Rex, Peter (2011). *1066: A New History of the Norman Conquest,* Amberley Publishing
Stenton, Frank. *Anglo-Saxon England (Oxford History of England)*

Poole, A.L. *From Domesday Book to Magna Carta 1087-1216 (Oxford History of England)*

Ackroyd, Peter (2012). *Foundation (History of England Volume 1),* Pan

Starkey, David (2011). *Crown and Country,* HarperPress

Stenton, Frank (1965). *The Bayeux Tapestry,* Phaidon Publishers

Bartlett, Robert. *England under the Norman and Angevin Kings 1075-1225*

Rowley, Trevor (2010). *Norman England (Shire Living Histories),* Shire

Rud, Mogens (2004). *The Bayeux Tapestry,* Christian Eilers Publishers

Neveux, Francois (2008). *A Brief History of the Normans (Brief Histories),* Robinson

Hindley, Geoffrey (2006). *A Brief History of the Anglo-Saxons (Brief Histories),* Robinson

English Heritage. *Battle Abbey and Battlefield Guidebook*

English Heritage. *Pevensey Castle Guidebook*

Historic Royal Palaces. *The Tower of London Guidebook*

Oxford Dictionary of National Biography. *Harold II*

Oxford Dictionary of National Biography. *William I*

Oxford Dictionary of National Biography. *Edward the Confessor*

Oxford Dictionary of National Biography. *Harald Hardrada*

Oxford Dictionary of National Biography. *Edgar Ætheling*

Barlow, Frank. *Edward the Confessor (Yale English Monarchs),* Yale University Press.

Online Resources

http://www.hs-augsburg.de/~harsch/Chronologia/Lspost11/Bayeux/bay_tama.html

About the Author

Charlie Fenton is currently studying history at the University of Kent, where she specialises in Medieval and Early Modern History. She is the author of Perseverance, a novel about Anne Boleyn, and runs the blog *Through the Eyes of Anne Boleyn*.

She is well known to members of the Tudor Society as the regular book reviewer and regularly writes for Tudor Life magazine.

Henry VIII's Health

in a nutshell

History "In a Nutshell" Series

KYRA KRAMER

ISBN: 978-84-944574-2-5

Tudor histories are rife with "facts" about Henry VIII's life and health, but, as a medical anthropologist **Kyra Kramer** has learned, one should never take those "facts" at face value.

In **Henry VIII's Health in a Nutshell**, Kramer highlights the various health issues that Henry suffered throughout his life, based on modern medical findings. Kramer gives the reader a new understanding of Henry VIII's health difficulties, and provides new insights into their possible causes.

Thomas Cranmer
in a nutshell

ISBN: 978-84-943721-3-1

History
"In a Nutshell"
Series

BETH VON STAATS

In **Thomas Cranmer in a Nutshell**, **Beth von Staats** discusses the fascinating life of **Thomas Cranmer**, from his early education, through his appointment to Archbishop of Canterbury, his growth in confidence as a reformer, the writing of two versions of the English Book of Common Prayer and eventually to his imprisonment, recantations and execution.

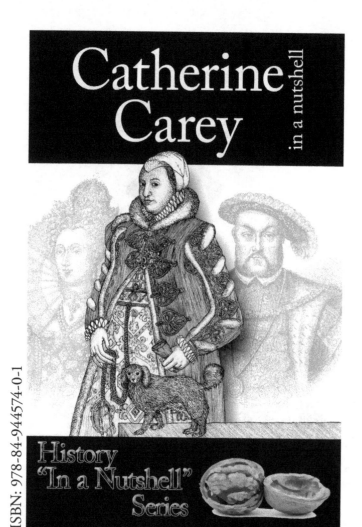

Catherine Carey
in a nutshell

ISBN: 978-84-944574-0-1

History
"In a Nutshell"
Series

ADRIENNE DILLARD

Catherine Carey in a Nutshell examines the life of Catherine Carey, daughter of Mary Boleyn, from the controversy surrounding her paternity through her service to Henry VIII's queens, the trials of life in Protestant exile during the Tudor era, and the triumphant return of the Knollys family to the glittering court of the Virgin Queen. This book brings together what is known about one of Queen Elizabeth I's most trusted and devoted ladies for the first time in one concise, easy-to-read book.

Sweating Sickness

in a nutshell

ISBN: 978-15-009962-2-2

History "In a Nutshell" Series

CLAIRE RIDGWAY

In **Sweating Sickness in a Nutshell**, **Claire Ridgway** examines what the historical sources say about the five epidemics of the mystery disease which hit England between 1485 and 1551, and considers the symptoms, who it affected, the treatments, theories regarding its cause and why it only affected English people.

Whitehall Palace

in a nutshell

ISBN: 978-84-944893-5-8

History "In a Nutshell" Series

PHILIP ROBERTS

In **Whitehall Palace in a Nutshell**, researcher and author *Philip Roberts* delves into the history of England's most important and significant lost building, a palace which had 2000 rooms and covered 23 acres in its heyday.

Using his unprecedented connections, Philip has been able to gain access to the historical places in Whitehall Palace which still exist today, many of which are not open to public access.

Philip Roberts, a member of the Mary Rose Trust Information Group Team for well over 20 years, has a passion for Tudor re-enactment and educating people about history.

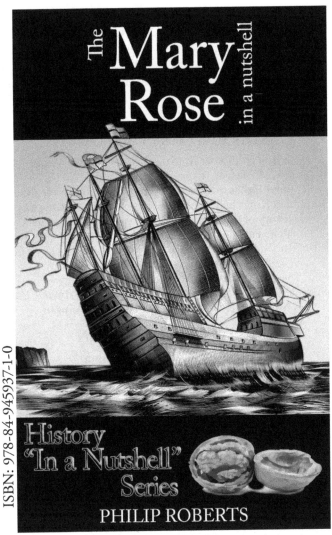

The **Mary Rose** in a nutshell

History "In a Nutshell" Series

PHILIP ROBERTS

ISBN: 978-84-945937-1-0

Henry VIII's prized flagship sank in 1545 under the watchful eye of the king himself. With it, over 500 men tragically lost their lives. Four hundred and thirty-seven years later, the ship was brought back to the surface and an intense conservation effort was begun.

In **The Mary Rose in a Nutshell**, researcher and author **Philip Roberts** delves into the history of England's most important historical find, the only Tudor ship in the world, containing artefacts unequalled anywhere else.

HISTORY IN A NUTSHELL SERIES

Sweating Sickness - **Claire Ridgway**
Thomas Cranmer - **Beth von Staats**
Henry VIII's Health - **Kyra Kramer**
Catherine Carey - **Adrienne Dillard**

The Pyramids - **Charlotte Booth**
The Mary Rose - **Philip Roberts**
Whitehall Palace - **Philip Roberts**

NON FICTION HISTORY

Anne Boleyn's Letter from the Tower - **Sandra Vasoli**
Jasper Tudor - **Debra Bayani**
Tudor Places of Great Britain - **Claire Ridgway**
Illustrated Kings and Queens of England - **Claire Ridgway**
A History of the English Monarchy - **Gareth Russell**
The Fall of Anne Boleyn - **Claire Ridgway**
George Boleyn: Tudor Poet, Courtier & Diplomat - **Ridgway & Cherry**
The Anne Boleyn Collection - **Claire Ridgway**
The Anne Boleyn Collection II - **Claire Ridgway**
Two Gentleman Poets at the Court of Henry VIII - **Edmond Bapst**
A Mountain Road - **Douglas Weddell Thompson**

HISTORICAL FICTION

The Devil's Chalice - **D.K.Wilson**
Falling Pomegranate Seeds - **Wendy J. Dunn**
Struck with the Dart of Love: Je Anne Boleyn 1 - **Sandra Vasoli**
Truth Endures: Je Anne Boleyn 2 - **Sandra Vasoli**
The Colour of Poison - **Toni Mount**
The Colour of Gold - **Toni Mount**
The Colour of Cold Blood - **Toni Mount**
Phoenix Rising - **Hunter S. Jones**
Cor Rotto - **Adrienne Dillard**
The Claimant - **Simon Anderson**

CHILDREN'S BOOKS

All about Richard III - **Amy Licence**
All about Henry VII - **Amy Licence**
All about Henry VIII - **Amy Licence**
Tudor Tales William at Hampton Court - **Alan Wybrow**

PLEASE LEAVE A REVIEW

If you enjoyed this book, *please* leave a review at the book
seller where you purchased it. There is no better way to thank
the author and it really does make a huge difference!
Thank you in advance.

Lightning Source UK Ltd.
Milton Keynes UK
UKHW03f1017230318
319940UK00006B/113/P